START LIVING
FOREVER

Understanding the eternality of your personal time.

Max Everlast

CONTENTS

Introduction

Start Living Forever: An Overview

In the vast realm of human existence, time bears a unique duality. From the moment of our birth to the present day, and then from this very instant until our final breath, lies a continuum that transcends the simple measures of calendars and clocks.

There is an intriguing paradox about our personal perception of life: the enigma of non-existence. Imagine trying to recall a time before you were born; it's an impossible task. This void, this absence of memory or perception, is the closest understanding we have of non-existence. Similarly, after we pass away, there is no conscious awareness to comprehend an 'after'. The span between our birth and the present moment, regardless of how many years that encompasses, feels profound and infinite. Whether we are in the tender years of youth, the reflective years of old age, or somewhere in the midst of life, the duration always feels eternal.

This sensation persists when we think about the time we have left; whether it's decades or mere days, it possesses a quality of infinity. In this light, our individual existence, framed by the incomprehensible voids before birth and after death, feels, for all intents and purposes, eternal.

This book dives deeper into this perception of the eternal stretches both behind and ahead of us, emphasizing the intricate relationship between chronology and cognition.

Time is a concept that, despite its ubiquity in our lives, remains largely enigmatic. From the relentless ticking of a clock to the changing seasons, it governs our very existence, marking milestones from birth to death.

Ancient civilizations had their interpretations of time, often aligning their understanding with the natural world. The rising and setting sun, phases of the moon, and changing tides offered them a way to measure days, months, and years. However, these measurements were merely attempts to grasp something much more profound: the intangible flow of moments.

Scientists, too, have wrestled with time. Albert Einstein's theory of relativity shattered traditional notions, suggesting that time isn't universal but relative, bending and stretching depending on speed and gravity. It introduced the idea that time, as we perceive it, might be vastly different from its objective reality.

Philosophers have pondered on it deeply, asking questions like "What is the present?" or "Does the past, once gone, exist in any real sense?". These musings shed light on the fluidity of time, suggesting it might be more of a mental construct than a tangible entity.

Our Perception: The Heart of Eternality

At the heart of our engagement with time is our perception. This chapter isn't merely an exploration of time as an external concept but a deep dive into how each individual experiences it.

Consider childhood, for instance. Summer vacations felt endless. A single day filled with adventures, games, and discoveries seemed to stretch on forever. But as adults, years seem to fly by in a blur. This discrepancy isn't due to the objective passage of time but our perception of it. But what molds this perception?

Neuroscientists have uncovered fascinating insights about our brain's relationship with time. The density of experiences, novelty, and the amount of information processed can stretch or shrink our perception of time. For instance, in life-threatening situations, when our brain goes into overdrive, time appears to slow down, a phenomenon many have reported during accidents.

This malleability of perception plays into the theory of the eternality of personal time. If our understanding and experience of time can stretch or compress based on internal and external factors, it's not far-fetched to believe that the time between our birth and now, and the now until our death, can feel eternal.

Moreover, our memories play a significant role in this perception. The way we recall events, the emotions attached to them, and the narratives we construct all contribute to our personal timeline. These memories, both vivid and hazy, create a continuum of experiences, adding depth to our existence.

As we delve deeper into the chapters ahead, we'll uncover layers to our relationship with time, drawing from science, philosophy, and personal anecdotes. The journey aims to offer not just an understanding but a profound appreciation of the moments we live, encouraging readers to view their lives through the lens of eternity.

At its core, this book doesn't just explore the concept of time; it's an invitation to reflect, to pause, and to deeply engage with the present. Because in understanding the eternality of our personal time, we might just find a richer, more fulfilling way to live.

CHAPTER 1

Birth: The Start of Our Eternal Journey

Time Before Birth: The Grand Nothingness

Imagine the universe's vast expanse: galaxies spinning, stars igniting, and the infinite void stretching beyond comprehension. Before your arrival into this cosmic dance, a multitude of events unfolded. Dinosaurs once claimed dominion over the Earth, great empires rose and fell in their quest for glory, and stars erupted in celestial fury, only to be reborn from stardust. This epic prologue to your existence, dense with history and change, is paradoxically perceived as a blank canvas— a grand nothingness in your personal narrative.

This perception raises a profound question: Does the time before our birth, which we didn't witness, actually exist in our personal timeline? It echoes the philosophical conundrum: "If a tree falls in a forest with no one around, does it make a sound?" In this context, do the eons preceding our existence bear relevance to our personal perception of time?

Our understanding of time is inextricably linked to consciousness. It's through consciousness that events gain significance, form memories, and foster anticipation. Prior to our birth, without our consciousness to acknowledge it, time in our personal story remains abstract, almost a non-entity.

The Moment of Consciousness: The Dawn of Eternity

The inception of individual consciousness is veiled in enigma. When does this profound awakening begin? Is it marked by the first heartbeat resonating within the womb, the inaugural cry piercing through the silence of birth, or the initial dreams weaving through a young mind? The onset of this consciousness signifies the commencement of our eternal journey.

This emergence isn't instantaneous but unfolds progressively. In its earliest days, an infant lacks a defined sense of 'self' or 'other.' There's no distinction between self and the external environment. However, as weeks merge into months, a gradual awakening occurs. The infant starts discerning patterns, forming rudimentary memories, and embarking on the lifelong odyssey of learning.

Each instance, each sensation during these formative stages, adds layers to our perception and understanding of the world, and consequently, time itself. Every new experience, every emotional and sensory input contributes to the expansive nature of life, lending a sense of infinity to our existence. According to the theory of the eternality of personal time, it's this depth and richness of experiences that imbue our lives with a sensation of endlessness.

Life's Firsts: A Catalogue of Eternities

The initial experiences of life hold a pivotal role in our timelines. First words, hesitant steps, the inaugural day of school—these milestones are indelibly etched in our memory. Their significance lies in their novelty; they are moments of profound discovery, transition, and growth. Each 'first' is akin to a portal to previously unexplored realms, each revelation stretching our perception of time.

Consider the first time you savored the sweetness of ice cream or the initial encounter with the softness of falling snow. Such moments seemed to stretch beyond their temporal bounds, didn't they? Filled with awe and wonder, these experiences contribute significantly to our perception of the eternal nature of our lives.

As we journey from birth, evolving from infancy to childhood, our grasp of time undergoes transformation. An eternity to a child eagerly anticipating their next birthday may seem but a fleeting instant to an adult. Yet, it's within these early years, brimming with discoveries, emotions, and myriad 'firsts,' that the foundation of our eternal journey is laid.

The Evolving Perception of Time

As children grow, their perception of time begins to shift. The once seemingly endless summer days start to take on a more definitive rhythm. The concept of 'tomorrow' or 'next week' starts to hold meaning. This evolving perception is a dance between growing cognitive abilities and an expanding repertoire of experiences.

Neurological studies suggest that our brain's development directly influences how we perceive time. As children, with fewer reference points and a narrower scope of experiences, each new day is a significant fraction of their life. Contrastingly, as adults, with a multitude of days behind us, individual days diminish in their relative significance, hence the feeling that time accelerates as we age.

This development is also mirrored in how children and adults approach and understand the concept of future. For a young child, the future is a hazy, distant reality, barely grasping beyond the immediate or the next exciting event. As we grow, our ability to project ourselves into the future, to plan, anticipate, and envision, becomes more sophisticated, altering our engagement with the concept of time.

Memory and Time

Our memories play a critical role in shaping our perception of time. Early childhood memories, though often fragmentary, form the backbone of our temporal understanding. The vividness of these memories, the emotions they evoke, and the narratives we construct around them greatly influence how we perceive the past and, in turn, our sense of the eternal nature of our lives.

The brain's ability to recall and relive past experiences allows us to traverse time mentally. This ability not only connects us to our past but also helps us to forecast and imagine the future. It's this unique human capacity to journey through time in our minds that contributes to the sense of an ongoing, eternal narrative.

As we progress from birth, growing from infants to toddlers to children, our understanding and perception of time evolve. What feels like an eternity for a child waiting for their next birthday might feel like a fleeting moment for an adult. But it's these early years, filled with discoveries, emotions, and 'firsts,' that lay the foundation for our eternal journey.

As we delve deeper into the chapters ahead, we'll explore these facets of memory and time, uncovering how they intertwine to create our unique perception of the temporal journey of life.

CHAPTER 2

The "Now": Our Eternal Present

The Mirage of Linear Time

Life, as we perceive it, seems to unfold on a timeline. Birth leads to experiences, which in turn lead to the inevitable end. This linear progression — past, present, and future — forms the backbone of our existence. But is this linearity just a construct, a convenient way for our minds to catalog events?

Science and philosophy concur on one truth: the only tangible reality is the present. The past exists as memories, and the future as anticipations. But both are experienced in the 'now.' Think of your most cherished memory. That very reminiscing is occurring in the present. The same goes for future aspirations. It's a mental projection happening right now.

Living in the Moment: The Power of Presence

Ancient wisdom from various cultures, and even modern therapeutic practices, extol the virtues of living in the moment. Being 'present' is not just a philosophical idea; it has tangible benefits. A fully engaged mind perceives the world with heightened clarity. Sounds resonate deeper, colors pop with vibrancy, and emotions become more palpable. These moments of intense presence give life its depth and richness, stretching each second into an eternity.

Mindfulness and meditation practices anchor this concept. They teach the brain to be here, now. The ruminations of the past or anxieties of the future fade, leaving only the immersive present. This grounding in the present moment, as countless practitioners can attest, provides a sense of peace, clarity, and a perception of time's eternal nature.

Memory, Anticipation, and the Eternal Present

One of the marvels of human cognition is its intricate dance with time. Memories, those vivid recollections of bygone moments, play out in the theater of the present mind. The scent of a childhood meal, the sound of a lullaby, or the touch of a loved one — these aren't time-traveling experiences but reconstructions in the current moment.

Anticipation operates similarly. Whether it's the thrill of an upcoming vacation or the nervousness before a significant event, these feelings and imaginations are constructed in the present. This continuous playback and projection underscore the profound truth that our existence, in all its depth and dimension, is firmly rooted in the 'now'.

The Stretching and Shrinking of the Present

Our perception of the present moment isn't static; it's malleable, shaped by myriad factors. Engrossment in a beloved activity, like reading a gripping novel or painting, can warp our sense of time, making hours feel like fleeting moments. In contrast, moments of heightened anxiety or anticipation can stretch seconds into what feels like hours.

Neuroscience offers insights into this phenomenon. In adrenaline-charged situations, the brain can go into overdrive, processing information at an accelerated pace, which can make external events seem to move in slow motion. On the other hand, repetitive or monotonous tasks can dull our cognitive senses, making time feel sluggish.

The relativity of our present experience is both a marvel and a mystery, pointing to the vast potential within our minds to shape our reality.

The Depth of Now: An Ever-present Ocean

While we often perceive the 'now' as a mere point on the timeline of our life, it is more aptly described as a vast ocean in which we're constantly submerged. Each wave, each ripple in this ocean, represents our experiences, thoughts, and emotions. Some waves are calm and serene, while others are turbulent and intense.

This oceanic 'now' is where life unfolds in all its beauty and chaos. By diving deeper into these waters, by truly experiencing each wave, we gain a richer understanding of our existence and the eternal nature of the present.

The 'now', far from being a transient blip, is a continuous, dynamic tapestry of experiences, emotions, and perceptions. It is in this eternal present that we live, love, suffer, dream, and ultimately exist. By recognizing and embracing the profound depth of each moment, we not only enrich our lives but also touch the very essence of eternity.

In subsequent chapters, we'll explore the mechanisms, practices, and life events that further deepen our engagement with the present and guide us on our eternal journey through time.

CHAPTER 3

Relationships: The Timeless Bonds We Forge

Introducing the Timeless Nature of Bonds

Life, in its essence, is not solely comprised of moments we experience in isolation. Our journey through the eternality of personal time intertwines beautifully with the bonds we form and nurture. Whether it be the steadfast love of family, the unwavering loyalty of friends, the passion in romantic relationships, or even the brief yet meaningful encounters with strangers, these connections don't just exist in the moment. They resonate, echoing through our perception of time, making certain moments feel infinite and others fleeting.

The First Connection: Parent and Child

The cornerstone of human relationships, the bond between a parent and a child, is where our understanding of time first begins to take shape. The safety of a mother's womb, the rhythm of a father's heartbeat - these are the very first interactions we experience. They're not just the foundations of love, but also our nascent comprehension of the continuum of existence.

Consider a child: to them, the hours their parents are away at work can feel like a small eternity. Yet, the embrace upon return, the warmth, and the shared laughter make those elongated hours pale in comparison. Such is the strength of this connection.

Think back to the tales told by parents at bedtime, of their own childhood, of heroes and heroines, of lessons learned. These stories, while from a time before our own existence, become integrated into our understanding of the past, making the events almost tangible, bridging the gap between generations, and emphasizing the timelessness of this bond.

Friendships: The Chronicles of Shared Time

As the sands of time flow and we venture out, we form another set of invaluable bonds – friendships. These relationships, born out of shared experiences, mutual interests, and deep understanding, carry a unique temporal magic. Remember the days of youth: the seemingly endless summers, the adventures, the shared secrets whispered under the blanket of night.

Yet, it's not just the length of time spent with friends but the depth of shared moments that renders them timeless. With true friends, distances and durations of separation become irrelevant. Reunions feel like resuming a paused conversation, a testament to the enduring nature of genuine connections.

Romantic Bonds: Eternities in Heartbeats

The world of romance, with its highs and lows, is a clear testament to the malleability of our perception of time. The exhilaration of newfound love, where moments of waiting can feel interminable, to the settled comfort of long-term relationships where years blend seamlessly, forming a rich tapestry of shared experiences.

There are moments where time appears to halt - a first kiss under a starlit sky, holding hands, feeling two heartbeats sync. Then there are periods, often challenging, where time drags, testing the bond. Yet, through the valleys and peaks of romantic endeavors, what becomes evident is the profound effect such connections have on our personal timelines.

Loss and Longing: The Paradox of Absence

Delving into the realm of relationships mandates confronting the inevitable - loss. It's a cruel twist, where the absence of a loved one can distort time in unimaginable ways. The days after a loss can stretch on, with grief making each second weigh heavily. Memories, both fresh and old, play out in the theater of the mind, oscillating between feeling immediate and achingly distant.

Yet, within this painful paradox lies a profound realization. The very fact that we feel such temporal distortions is testament to the depth of bonds formed. And as the theory of the eternality of personal time suggests, our loved ones embark on their own timeless journeys, their legacies continuing to influence our timeline, reminding us of the interconnectedness of existence.

It is clear, relationships play a pivotal role in how we navigate the river of time. They anchor us, provide context, offer joy, challenge, and often, lessons. Time, then, is not merely a solitary journey. It is a shared odyssey, a dance of souls through the ages.

The intricate tapestry of our lives is woven with threads of moments, some ours, some borrowed from those we hold dear. These shared experiences, emotions, and memories transcend the mere ticking of the clock, crafting a narrative rich in depth, emotion, and eternality.

In subsequent chapters, we will delve further into other elements that shape our timeless journey, exploring the myriad ways our lives are rendered both ephemeral and eternal.

CHAPTER 4

Milestones: Marking Eternities in Our Journey

Understanding Milestones: More than Just Dates

In the theater of life, milestones stand out as grand acts, moments that punctuate our narrative with vivid intensity. These aren't mere dates on a calendar but soulful symphonies of experiences that resonate deeply within our being. At a superficial level, they might seem like events that come and go, but their reverberations are felt long after, echoing through the corridors of our memories, reminding us of their significance.

But what truly constitutes a milestone? Is it the event itself, or is it the profound metamorphosis it triggers within us? It's the latter. Milestones are transformative experiences that shift our paradigms, recalibrate our perceptions, and often, redefine our very essence.

Childhood Milestones: The Foundations of Self

Our life's symphony begins with the soft notes of childhood milestones. These moments might appear small in the grand scheme of life, but their magnitude in shaping our psyche is unparalleled. The thrill of uttering the first word, the adventure of the first step, the mixed emotions of the first day at school - all of these create ripples in the fabric of our nascent self.

Remember the sheer exhilaration of riding a bicycle without support for the first time? Or the first time you were praised for a drawing or a small achievement? Such instances might seem trivial in retrospect, but in the moment, they were transformative, expanding our universe, making us feel boundless and eternal.

Adolescence to Adulthood: Discoveries and Realizations

The crescendo of life's music amplifies during the transition from adolescence to adulthood. This phase is a whirlwind of emotions, laden with discoveries, realizations, aspirations, and often, disillusionments. The world appears larger, possibilities seem endless, and the path ahead, though uncertain, is thrilling.

Consider the myriad emotions experienced during your first heartbreak or the pride swelling within as you donned your graduation robe. The anxiety and excitement of the first job interview, the joy of the first paycheck, the introspection following the first major failure - all these moments, while diverse, share a common thread. They pull and stretch our perception of time, making it malleable, fluid.

Adulthood: Celebrations, Challenges, and Reflections

As the cadence of life mellows into adulthood, milestones take on a nuanced shade. Now, they are not just about personal growth but also about relationships, responsibilities, and retrospection. The euphoria of one's wedding day, the indescribable emotion when holding one's child for the first time, the pride of purchasing a home – these milestones etch deep imprints on our soul.

Even the challenges, like navigating the intricacies of parenthood or weathering professional storms, while daunting, become milestones of resilience, teaching us the timeless lesson of perseverance.

Golden Years: Reminiscence and Legacy

As the twilight years approach, milestones morph into reflections, reminiscences, and legacies. It's no longer just about forging ahead but looking back, understanding the journey, cherishing the highs, learning from the lows, and pondering on the legacy one wishes to leave behind.

In the eyes of an elderly individual, past milestones don't feel dated. Narrating tales from their youth, there's a gleam in their eyes, a vigor in their voice, making yesteryears feel like recent memories. Such is the power of milestones; they blur the lines between the past and present, making moments feel eternally fresh.

Milestones, in essence, are not merely chronological markers. They are emotional, psychological, and spiritual anchors that lend depth and dimension to our journey. Each milestone, be it joyous or challenging, adds a unique thread to the tapestry of our existence.

When we step back and look at this tapestry, we don't just see events. We see a mosaic of emotions, decisions, growth, and transformations. Through milestones, our life becomes less about the number of days lived and more about the eternities experienced within those days.

In the forthcoming chapters, we will delve deeper into other facets of life that, much like milestones, transform our linear journey into an expansive, eternal adventure.

CHAPTER 5

Embracing Eternity in the Golden Years

Sunsets of Wisdom

The term "golden years" isn't merely a euphemism for old age. It captures the essence of a lifetime drenched in experiences, insights, triumphs, and lessons. Sunsets during these times gleam with a unique brilliance, reflective of the accumulated wisdom of years gone by.

But can embracing the Eternality of Personal Time elevate the experience of these years? Can this concept enrich the autumn of life, making every moment seem more profound, more connected, more eternal?

The Depth of the Current Moment: Time's Unchanging Promise

One might think that as age advances, time speeds up, reducing the breadth of experiences. But delve deeper, and one realizes that the richness of the present moment remains unaltered, regardless of age. A child's wonder at a fluttering butterfly and an elder's reflection on the same scene both capture eternity in their unique ways.

Every heartbeat, every sigh, every laugh is an embodiment of an eternal moment, waiting to be embraced, irrespective of one's age. Time, in its essence, is a continuum, never discriminating between the young or the old, offering infinite possibilities to all.

Revisiting a Lifetime of Infinite Moments

Memories, when viewed through the lens of eternity, do not fade or become distant but rather take on a timeless quality. The past, in its entirety, becomes a repository of eternal moments that continue to influence and enrich the present.

- Remember the innocent mischief of childhood, when hours seemed like days?

- Recall the heady excitement of young love, where the wait between meetings felt like eons, yet the moments spent together seemed all too fleeting?

- Think about the challenges faced, the battles won, the lessons learned. Each hurdle, each victory, though in the past, feels as fresh and as influential as ever.

Such is the power of revisiting memories with the awareness of their timeless nature. Every emotion, every experience, once lived, becomes an indelible part of our eternal narrative.

Charting the Future with a New Perspective

Contrary to popular belief, the golden years aren't just about reminiscing. They're also about envisioning, exploring, and evolving. Recognizing the eternal nature of personal time means understanding that every coming day, irrespective of one's age, holds the promise of infinite experiences.

- It's an invitation to explore uncharted territories, maybe a forgotten hobby or a newfound passion.

- It's an opportunity to form bonds, to reconnect with old friends or to discover new kindred spirits.

- It's a chance to mentor, to guide, to pass on one's wisdom, ensuring that one's legacy resonates through time.

Today's Eternity: The Joy of the Golden Present

The golden years, with their inherent wisdom, present a unique blend of retrospection and anticipation. But they also emphasize the beauty of 'now.' The aroma of freshly brewed coffee, the mellifluous chirping of birds, or the sheer tranquility of a silent evening— these seemingly mundane moments hold within them the essence of eternity.

This phase of life serves as a gentle reminder that while memories are precious and the future holds promise, it's the present that truly matters. Each moment lived in these years is a testament to the journey undertaken, the battles fought, the love shared, and the wisdom earned.

The golden years, when seen through the prism of the Eternality of Personal Time, become a vibrant mosaic of the past, present, and future. Each day becomes an opportunity, each moment a treasure, each experience a step closer to understanding the grand tapestry of existence.

With this renewed perspective, these years aren't just a culmination but a continuation, a phase where every second holds the promise of eternity. As the sun sets, casting its golden glow, it's a reminder that while days end, the dance with eternity continues, celebrating the timeless beauty of life.

CHAPTER 6

Navigating Eternity Amidst Health Challenges

Embracing Eternity

When waves of health challenges crash upon the shores of one's existence, the resulting turbulence can be disorienting. Yet, amidst these unpredictable currents, many find the strength to anchor themselves, searching for and often discovering a glimmer of light even in the darkest caverns of discomfort.

The Eternality of Personal Time Theory provides such an anchoring concept, suggesting that time's depth remains unyielding, even when our physical or mental well-being might waver. To truly appreciate this perspective during times of health challenges requires a journey both inward and outward.

The Distorted Lens of Pain and The Unchanging Nature of Time

Pain and discomfort, whether physical or emotional, have a unique way of stretching our perception of time. Each second can feel elongated, each hour like an eternity. Yet, it's crucial to discern the difference between our perception of time and its intrinsic nature.

While health issues can slow down our activities and make days seem longer, the essence of every moment remains just as vast and profound.

Rediscovering Self: The Inner Sanctuary

Health challenges often compel a retreat from the external world. This retreat, though sometimes involuntary, offers a unique opportunity to embark on an inward odyssey. Within the mind lies a universe as vast as the one outside, waiting to be navigated.

Reconnecting with oneself can lead to revelations, healing, and even transformations. Engaging in introspective or creative activities can help map out this inner terrain, providing avenues for self-expression and understanding.

Deepened Relationships: Bonds Beyond Physicality

Health struggles bring to the surface the raw, unfiltered essence of human relationships. These challenges, by their very nature, demand vulnerability, leading to profound conversations that often transcend the superficial.

Engaging in these dialogues, sharing fears, aspirations, and reminiscences, can deepen bonds in unprecedented ways. It's a reminder that relationships are the bridges we construct over the turbulent rivers of life, helping us navigate its unpredictable courses.

The Power of Empathy & Profound Understanding

Walking the path of health challenges amplifies one's capacity for empathy. Such experiences, while individual, resonate with universal emotions, fostering a deep understanding of the human condition.

This newfound sensitivity can open doors to deeper connections with art, literature, cinema, and most importantly, with people. Sharing this profound understanding can become a beacon of hope and solace for others navigating similar challenges.

Intentionally Sailing the Expansive Sea of Time

The recognition of time's endless depth can lead to purposeful engagement with each moment. Despite physical constraints, one can dive deep into the ocean of the present, savoring its richness.

Activities like meditation, deep breathing, or even listening to calming music can be a bridge to the present's depth. Take a trip down memory lane, revisit cherished memories. Each reminiscence is an eternal moment in itself. Visualize the future, not just for yourself but for your loved ones. These visions can be grounding and therapeutic amidst the tempests of health challenges.

Crafting a Timeless Legacy

The legacy we leave behind isn't solely composed of physical achievements or tangible assets. It's intricately woven with the stories we share, the wisdom we impart, and the emotions we evoke.

Health challenges, while limiting in some respects, provide unique opportunities to craft legacies that transcend the confines of time. In sharing, expressing, and connecting, one creates ripples that reverberate through eternity.

Embracing Eternality Amidst Mental Struggles

Living with mental health issues can sometimes feel like being trapped in a labyrinth. The walls seem high, the paths convoluted, and every turn feels uncertain. The weight of the mind can distort our perception of time, making moments of despair feel eternal. Yet, the Eternality of Personal Time Theory has the potential to shine light into these dark corridors, offering a transformative perspective on time and the depth of each moment.

Mental health struggles, though undoubtedly challenging, do not diminish the vastness and depth of each individual's personal time. By embracing the Eternality of Personal Time Theory, it's possible to find pockets of clarity, hope, and connection even within the complex maze of the mind.

Remember, each moment, regardless of its emotional texture, holds within it an endless expanse of experiences, lessons, and growth.

Health challenges, whether physical, mental or both, reshape the contours of our existence. But with the Eternality of Personal Time Theory as a compass, one can navigate these altered landscapes with an awareness that transcends the immediate, delving into the depths of each moment with grace and intention.

As our journey continues, we will explore how larger societal and global narratives influence our individual perceptions of time and eternity, revealing the interconnectedness of our personal timelines with the world at large.

CHAPTER 7

Societal and Global Rhythms: The Greater Clocks That Shape Us

Beyond Personal Timelines

While our personal milestones deeply influence our perception of time, we are also part of a larger community, society, and world. Collective events – be it cultural festivals, historical occurrences, or global phenomena – play a crucial role in shaping our temporal experiences.

Cultural Festivals and Traditions: Time's Recurring Celebrations

Every culture has its own set of festivals and traditions, which often come around annually. These serve as communal milestones, marking the passage of time in a grand, celebratory manner.

Think about the anticipation and preparation for a major holiday in your culture. The rhythm of these celebrations, their predictability, and the collective joy they bring, anchor our years, providing both continuity and a cyclical perception of time.

Historical Occurrences: Echoes from the Past

Major historical events, even if they occurred before our time, shape societal memory and influence our collective perception of time. Wars, revolutions, moments of great achievement, or even tragedies are remembered and commemorated.

For instance, consider how events like the moon landing, even for those born much later, create a sense of wonder and a marker in the timeline of human achievement. Such events, though not experienced firsthand, become part of our collective consciousness, adding depth and perspective to our individual timelines.

Global Phenomena: Shared Experiences Across Time Zones

The modern era, marked by globalization, has seen events that transcend borders and cultures. A FIFA World Cup final, the global response to climate change, or the shared anticipation of a lunar eclipse – these experiences stitch together diverse timelines, creating a shared tapestry of moments that resonate across continents.

The collective awe during space missions or the united resilience during global crises illustrates the power of shared experiences. They amplify moments, turning them into global memories that stand as testaments to human unity and connection.

Reflect on a moment when you were part of such a global event. The shared anticipation, the collective emotion, and the universal conversation that follows make these moments feel larger than life, stretching our sense of the present.

The Digital Age: Time Compression and Expansion

In the age of information, our relationship with time has transformed. Moments are captured, shared, and relived, altering our linear experience of time. The instantaneous nature of digital communication juxtaposed against the permanence of online memories creates a duality – making the recent feel distant and the distant feel palpably close.

Exploring this digital timeline offers insights into our evolving relationship with time. The immediate accessibility of information, the endurance of digital memories, and the global simultaneity fostered by the internet creates a dynamic and ever-shifting perception of time's flow.

Societal Progress and Innovations: The Future in the Present

With every passing decade, humanity inches closer to previously unimaginable futures. Breakthroughs in science, shifts in societal values, or technological innovations – each of these not only shape the future but redefine the present.

Reflect on the leaps of the past century: from the invention of the airplane to advancements in artificial intelligence. Each innovation, while heralding a new era, also reshapes our current moment, making it a nexus of past achievements and future possibilities.

Our perception of time, while deeply personal, is invariably linked to larger rhythms. From cultural celebrations to global phenomena, these collective experiences enrich our individual journeys, reminding us that our personal stories are but threads in the vast tapestry of time.

As we venture into the subsequent chapters, we will explore tools and philosophies that allow us to fully embrace and navigate this intricate interplay of personal and collective time, appreciating the beauty and depth of our shared voyage through eternity.

CHAPTER 8

The Psychology of Eternity: How Our Minds Grasp the Infinite

The Hunan Mind

The human mind is a vessel navigating the vast ocean of time, ceaselessly seeking the shores of understanding. In our quest for meaning, we confront the infinite — a concept as awe-inspiring as it is perplexing. The psychology of eternity examines how we, as finite beings, come to grips with the infinite nature of time and our own existence within it

The Perception of Infinity

Infinity is an abstract, often mathematical concept that stands in stark contrast to the tangible, measurable reality we inhabit. Yet, our consciousness is drawn to it, trying to reconcile the finite nature of our lives with the boundless continuum of eternity. This chapter explores how our brains process the vastness of forever and how this understanding influences our perception of life, death, and the purpose of our existence.

Cognitive Approaches to Eternity

Cognitive psychology delves into the mental processes involved in thinking about eternity. From the development of abstract thinking in children to the complex philosophical musings of adults, we are constantly expanding our cognitive maps to include not just the temporal but the eternal. We look at how individuals vary in their capacity to conceive of infinite time and how this influences their worldview and decision-making.

Emotional Response to the Eternal

The thought of eternity can elicit a powerful emotional response — from existential dread to sublime wonder. This chapter examines the spectrum of emotions associated with the eternal, and how these feelings shape our approach to life. The concept of eternity can be a source of comfort for some, offering a sense of continuity beyond the physical lifespan, while for others, it can be overwhelming, a reminder of our own insignificance in the face of the boundless

The Role of Culture and Religion

Our understanding of eternity is often framed by cultural narratives and religious doctrines. These systems of thought provide context and meaning, shaping our perceptions of an infinite timeline. By examining various cultural and religious interpretations of eternity, we gain insight into the myriad ways humanity has come to terms with the infinite.

The Eternal Now

Within the field of psychology, the concept of "the eternal now" suggests that our only true experience of time is the present moment. This chapter explores mindfulness and the practice of being fully engaged with the now, where the infinite seems to converge into a single point of experience. We investigate the therapeutic benefits of this perspective and how it might alleviate the anxiety associated with grasping the infinite.

The Fear of Infinity

For some, the concept of infinity is inherently tied to the fear of the unknown. This chapter delves into the psychological mechanisms behind this fear and how it can be both a source of existential angst and a catalyst for personal growth. We explore strategies to confront and embrace the uncertainty of eternity, and how doing so can lead to a richer, more accepting approach to life.

Psychological Time and Personal Eternity

Psychological time is our subjective experience of time's passage. This chapter contemplates how psychological time shapes our personal narrative of eternity. It discusses the elasticity of time perception — how moments can seem to stretch into infinity and years can pass in a blink — and how this subjective time influences our individual sense of an eternal self.

The concept of eternity stretches the boundaries of human understanding, challenging the very frameworks within which our minds operate. As we attempt to grasp the infinite, we embark on a journey that is as much about exploring the depths of our own psyche as it is about comprehending the eternal.

By understanding the psychology behind our perception of infinity, we gain not only insight into the nature of time and existence but also a greater awareness of the profound capabilities of our own minds. This chapter calls us to embrace the mystery of eternity as a gateway to deeper self-knowledge and a more meaningful engagement with life's temporal tapestry.

CHAPTER 9

Living in the Eternity: Strategies and Philosophies for an Immersive Life

Embracing the Timeless Journey

Now that we've explored the complexities and layers of time from personal and societal perspectives, the question arises: How do we live a life that's both meaningful and immersed in this understanding of eternal time? This chapter dives deep into the strategies and philosophies that can guide our daily existence.

Mindfulness: The Power of the Present

At the core of truly experiencing the eternality of life is the practice of mindfulness. By being fully present in each moment, we don't just observe time; we live it.

To fully grasp and engage with life's unending tapestry, we must embrace mindfulness in its purest form. This is not simply about observing the world around us but fully living within each fleeting moment.

Techniques like focused breathing amidst the rush of our daily routines or truly tasting and experiencing our food during meals can serve as anchors. Yet, beyond these acts, a deeper level of mindfulness arises from introspective practices. Journaling, meditation, or even simple solitary walks can amplify our connection to the present, making every moment resonate with clarity and depth.

Legacy Building: Crafting Eternities

Understanding our life as an eternal journey often brings forth the question of legacy. Pondering the vastness of time, we're faced with a reflection of our lasting impact. How do our actions, big or small, ripple through the ages?

Crafting a legacy is more than just monumental feats; it's in the daily decisions, the kindness we show, the passions we pursue, and the wisdom we share. Whether it's through artistic pursuits, community engagement, or mentorship, consciously aligning our actions with a sense of purpose ensures our legacies remain vibrant and impactful long after our immediate presence.

Temporal Fluidity: Moving Between Past, Present, and Future

An immersive life is not one that's just rooted in the present. It fluidly moves between memories of the past, experiences of the present, and aspirations for the future.

To fully immerse in the vast spectrum of time, one must be adept at navigating the memories of the past, the immediacies of the present, and the potentials of the future. Our histories, filled with lessons and cherished moments, should be honored.

Reflective practices, like journaling or revisiting old haunts, can be therapeutic, helping us cherish our past without being chained to it. Meanwhile, setting clear, adaptable visions for our future, without becoming overly rigid, provides direction and purpose, making the journey as rewarding as any imagined destination.

Embracing Change: The Only Constant

If time is eternal, then change is its most loyal companion. By embracing change, we align ourselves with the natural flow of life, although change itself, is often unpredictable in nature.

To be in harmony with life's flow, we must be willing to waltz with these winds of change. This means cultivating resilience that allows us to bounce back from life's inevitable setbacks. It also means constantly learning, growing, and evolving. By staying curious, seeking new experiences, and being open to the world's ever-changing nature, we ensure our dance through time remains dynamic and invigorating.

Connecting with Others: Shared Eternities

While our perception of time is personal, our lives are filled with shared moments. Cultivating and cherishing connections can amplify our experience of eternality.

This creates a vibrant mosaic of shared experiences, emotions, and insights. Deep, genuine connections with others not only add richness to our timeline but expand our understanding of existence's vastness. Engaging in shared projects, communal goals, or simply taking the time to truly listen to another's story allows us to explore and appreciate the numerous timelines converging with our own.

Life, with its intricate dance of moments, emotions, and experiences, offers us a chance to truly live eternally. By practicing mindfulness, building a legacy, fluidly navigating time, embracing change, and deeply connecting with others, we can immerse ourselves in the rich tapestry of existence. These strategies and philosophies are not mere tools but guiding lights, illuminating our path in this eternal journey.

In the chapters that follow, we'll explore the broader implications of this understanding, examining how societies, cultures, and humanity at large can benefit from recognizing and honoring the eternality of life.

CHAPTER 10

The Ripple Effect: How Embracing Eternality Can Shape Societies

From Individual to Collective

Our understanding of time's eternality, while deeply personal, has broad societal implications. As individuals come to appreciate and embody this sense of the eternal now, the ripples can be felt throughout communities, societies, and even civilizations. In this chapter, we'll delve into the transformative potential of such a paradigm shift.

A Compassionate Society: Empathy in the Eternal Frame

When we understand our lives as eternal journeys, we become more attuned to the experiences and struggles of others, fostering a deeper sense of empathy.

Envision a society wherein each soul comprehends its eternal journey. Such profound understanding organically magnifies empathy, realizing that every person we encounter has tales woven across time. This recognition nurtures profound connections, mutual respect, and heightened camaraderie.

Societies rooted in this ideology foster environments where shared experiences are not transient moments but impactful memories, leading communities towards cohesive, supportive, and uplifted existences.

Historical Reverence: Learning from the Eternal Past

When societies grasp the endless spectrum of time, the pages of history are no longer relics of the past but guiding lights for the present and future. This deep appreciation births institutions that are guardians of heritage—museums, libraries, cultural epicenters where bygone eras resonate vibrantly. Such societies are not just informed but enlightened, ensuring every leap forward is grounded in wisdom and sustainability.

Forward-Thinking Governance: Planning for the Eternal Future

Governments and leaders who embrace the concept of eternality are more likely to prioritize long-term benefits over short-term gains.

Imagine governance sculpted with an eternal lens. Such leadership transcends the immediate, embracing policies that prioritize the longevity of their civilizations. The emphasis shifts towards sustainable practices—from environment conservation to resource mindfulness—ensuring generations yet unborn inherit a world both bountiful and harmonious.

Education in these societies morphs into an ever-evolving realm, nurturing minds that value adaptability, lifelong learning, and an encompassing sense of global kinship.

Holistic Well-being: Health in the Eternal Paradigm

With an understanding of life's eternality, societies can prioritize holistic well-being, considering both physical and mental health.

In such communities, practices like meditation, yoga, and mindfulness are not alternatives but essentials, integrated into the very rhythm of life. Moreover, collective initiatives emerge, spotlighting emotional wellness, forging deeper social bonds, and amplifying mental health dialogues.

Economic Systems for Eternity: Beyond Short-Term Profits

An eternal perspective can lead to economic models that value sustainability, equitable growth, and long-term prosperity evolving beyond quick gains.

Here, growth is measured not in immediate profits but in sustainable prosperity. Such societies champion businesses that are harmonious with nature, equitable in practices, and visioned for longevity. Economic ventures in these realms become legacy projects, infrastructures, and initiatives envisioned to enrich countless generations.

Art and Culture: Expressing the Eternal Human Spirit

The arts become a medium to express, explore, and celebrate the eternal nature of human existence. Art, in its myriad forms, becomes the voice of the eternal spirit in these societies. It's not merely an expression but an exploration—a celebration of the timelessness of human existence.

Artworks, be it literature, music, or visual creations, resonate with themes that transcend temporal boundaries. Concurrently, cultural festivities emerge as grand orchestrations, seamlessly interweaving past traditions with present passions and future aspirations, crafting a collective symphony of memories and dreams.

When individuals embrace their eternal essence, the transformation is not isolated—it ripples, it resonates, and it revolutionizes societies at their core. This metamorphosis, profound and all-encompassing, breathes compassion into communities, wisdom into governance, holistic health into lifestyles, sustainability into economies, and timeless beauty into art and culture. As more individuals embark on their eternal journeys, the collective harmony has the potential to craft a world radiant in its connectedness, compassion, and consciousness—a world that honors its rich heritage while dreaming boundlessly into the future.

CHAPTER 11

The Science of Now - Time, Consciousness, and Quantum Realities

Unraveling Time's Tapestry

The theory of personal eternality doesn't just stand as a philosophical or spiritual beacon; it resonates with the pulsing heart of contemporary science. This chapter will bridge the gap between the abstractness of eternal time and the empirical evidence that supports it, journeying through the corridors of quantum mechanics, the mysteries of consciousness, and the latest research on mindfulness.

The Mind's Anchor to the Now

The quantum realm, a landscape where the usual rules of time and space are turned on their heads, hints at the timelessness of the universe. Quantum entanglement, a phenomenon Albert Einstein famously referred to as "spooky action at a distance," suggests that two particles can be inextricably linked in such a way that the state of one instantaneously influences the state of another, regardless of the distance separating them. This challenges the classical view of time as a linear flow, hinting at an interconnected reality where time is not as straightforward as our experiences suggest.

Entangling Time with Reality

Delving deeper into the rabbit hole, we encounter the concept of superposition, where particles exist in all possible states simultaneously until observed. This quantum behavior has tantalizing implications for our understanding of time, suggesting a reality that is far more malleable and eternal than previously imagined. The act of observation collapses this superposition into one state, the present moment, weaving the observer indelibly into the fabric of reality. This underlines the centrality of the 'now' – the eternal present – as a foundation of our experience of existence.

How Our Brains Encode Time

Turning from the vast cosmos to the human mind, we find consciousness presenting its own enigmas. Neuroscientific research is beginning to uncover how our brains perceive and construct time.

It's been proposed that our persistent sense of 'nowness' is a mental construct, a series of snapshots strung together by our consciousness to create the illusion of a continuous flow. If this is true, then each moment stands as its own eternity, an infinite point that our minds thread into the tapestry of time.

Techniques for Expanding the Now

Mindfulness and meditation practices have long been used to center oneself in the present moment. Modem research confirms that these practices can have profound effects on our brains, including changes in regions associated with memory, sense of self, and stress regulation. They can alter our perception of time, slowing it down and allowing us to live more fully in the now, appreciating each moment as a microcosm of eternity.

The Flow and Stretch of the Present

As we begin to understand the 'now' through the lens of science, we see that time may not just flow from the past to the future, but that the present is a field of possibilities, a vast ocean where every moment is a nexus of existence stretching out in every direction. This present moment, which we too often overlook, is not a mere point on a line but a doorway to eternity.

The Eternality of Personal Time Theory finds unexpected allies in the realms of quantum physics and neuroscience. These fields provide us with compelling evidence that the present moment holds a significance that transcends its fleeting nature, offering us a scientific foundation for a concept that has the power to transform how we live our lives.

In embracing the 'Science of Now', we embrace the boundless potential of our existence. Each moment is not a tick of the clock but a boundless landscape to explore, a realm where the past, present, and future coalesce into a singularity of experience. Here, in the science of now, we find not just theories and hypotheses but a call to live with an awareness that every second is a bridge to the infinite.

CHAPTER 12

Embracing Eternality for Tangible Positive Changes

Introduction to Real-World Applications

The Eternality of Personal Time Theory proposes a profound shift in perspective – that every individual lives within an eternal timeline. This notion, when truly embodied, can reshape every aspect of our lives, bringing clarity, depth, and fulfillment..

Improved Mindfulness and Presence

Every moment possesses its infinite value. Recognizing this can greatly amplify our presence:

Increased Productivity: Tasks, no matter how mundane, when approached with an eternal lens, demand our utmost dedication and precision. This elevated focus yields work that stands out not just in quality but in its resonant impact.

Enhanced Interpersonal Interactions: Every conversation, every shared laughter, every debated idea, when seen through the eternal prism, becomes a cherished imprint on our continuous timeline. This perspective transforms casual interactions into genuine engagements, sowing seeds of lasting connections.

Augmented Appreciation: An eternal awareness heightens our sensitivity towards life's minutiae. The first rays of dawn, the melody of a distant song, the aroma of a loved one's cooking - all metamorphose from fleeting moments to eternal memories.

Strengthened Relationships

If every shared moment is eternal, relationships take on a deeper resonance:

Rejuvenation of Bonds: Regularly reminiscing and cherishing shared experiences keeps relationships vibrant, emphasizing their eternal significance.

Communication Enhancement: Openly discussing aspirations, dreams, and fears, acknowledging that they too are eternal, leads to profound connections.

Legacy Building: The act of creating lasting memories ensures that the relationship leaves an indelible mark in the eternal timeline.

Enhanced Career Perspective

Aligning professional endeavors with the concept of eternity brings forth a deeper sense of purpose:

Value-Driven Endeavors: Recognizing the eternal impact of one's work encourages the pursuit of projects with long-term societal benefits.

Sustainable Thinking: An eternal perspective naturally gravitates towards sustainable and eco-friendly initiatives, as these have lasting positive effects.

Team Cohesion: Shared visions and goals, when seen as eternally impactful, foster unparalleled team unity.

Personal Growth and Development

Personal evolution is not just about milestones, but about eternally marking one's growth:

Continuous Learning: With an eternal mindset, there's no end to growth. This perspective fuels a constant hunger for knowledge and new skills.

Broadened Horizons: Immersing oneself in diverse experiences, knowing they contribute to one's eternal narrative, enriches one's worldview.

Legacy Mindset: The knowledge that personal achievements have an eternal ripple effect encourages the pursuit of meaningful goals.

Grieving and Healing

When grappling with loss, the eternal perspective offers unique solace:

Shared Grief: While the pain of loss is real, the understanding that loved ones continue to exist eternally in their own timeline brings comfort. They aren't truly gone; they continue their eternal journey.

Tribute to the Departed: Celebrating a loved one's life not as an end but as a continued existence in another dimension provides healing.

Healing Mechanism: Recognizing the eternal journey of each individual helps in accepting loss, turning grief into a celebration of the departed's eternal life.

Health and Self-care

Personal health decisions, when made with eternity in mind, become more profound:

Holistic Health: Understanding that well-being has an eternal impact encourages a balanced approach to mental and physical health.

Sustainable Habits: Habits and routines, when seen as contributing to an eternal state of well-being, are more likely to be sustainable and health-centric.

Mind-Body Harmony: Recognizing the importance of both mental peace and physical health in one's eternal journey ensures a harmonious life approach.

To truly integrate the Eternality of Personal Time Theory into one's life is to journey through each day with a heightened sense of purpose, passion, and profundity. Every decision, relationship, and endeavor becomes part of an endless tapestry, intricately woven with threads of eternal significance. Through this lens, life is not about the race to the finish but the beauty, depth, and intricacies of the journey itself.

CHAPTER 13

Harnessing the Law of Attraction within the Eternality of Personal Time

The Timeless Dance of Desire

Unifying the principles of the Eternality of Personal Time Theory with the well-regarded Law of Attraction forms a dynamic synergy. The Law of Attraction emphasizes the magnetic power of our thoughts and emotions to attract corresponding events. When combined with the limitless continuum of our personal time, this presents an opportunity for profound transformative experiences.

Infinite Canvas for Manifestation

The limitless expanse of our personal eternality offers an unending realm for manifestations.

Limitless Time: Temporal constraints can often be restrictive in our manifesting processes. The eternal perspective, however, grants us the grace of infinite time, encouraging patience and faith in the universe's timing.

Deepening Desires: Recognizing the infinite timeline intensifies the depth of our wishes, making them more than just fleeting yearnings but eternal imprints.

Amplifying Intentions through Eternality

Every intention, when viewed through the lens of eternity, carries more weight and vigor.

Resonance of Thoughts: Our every thought and wish, being eternally significant, vibrates powerfully within the universe, attracting corresponding outcomes with greater intensity.

Eternal Ripples: Understanding that our intentions cause eternal ripples can foster a more conscious and deliberate approach to manifesting. By realizing the eternal ripples our minds can generate, we approach our desires with a more conscious and deliberate intent, enhancing our manifestation power.

The Eternal Now - A Potent Manifestation Tool

The concept of the "eternal now" serves as a powerful tool in the Law of Attraction's arsenal. Our heightened present-moment awareness, amplified by its eternal importance, tunes our attracting power to its peak, with every emotion felt in the now echoing endlessly, shaping our reality with greater precision.

Heightened Awareness: By grounding ourselves in the present, which holds eternal importance, we fine-tune our awareness, making our attracting power more potent.

Living Vibrations: Every emotion felt in the present reverberates eternally, and aligning these emotions positively can significantly enhance manifestations.

The Interplay of Past, Present, Future in Attraction

In the vastness of personal eternality, past, present, and future are intertwined.

Healing the Past: By realigning our past narratives, viewing them as eternally influential, we can transform past traumas into lessons, thereby improving our current vibrational state.

Savoring the Present: By experiencing the present as a continuous, eternal moment, we maximize our positive vibrational alignment.

Crafting the Future: Envisioning our desired future, understanding its eternal impact, helps crystallize our manifestations.

The Art of Detachment in Eternity

Embracing the infinite nature of our existence, we learn the art of detachment—a key aspect of the Law of Attraction.

Flow of Eternity: With the knowledge that our desires will manifest in the expansive timeline of eternity, we can let go, trusting the universe's flow.

Releases and Returns: In the boundless realm of personal time, what we release often returns in unexpected, harmonious ways, reinforcing the importance of detachment.

Recalibrating with the Eternal Cycle

Our eternal journey offers continuous chances for realignment and manifestation.

Revisiting Desires: Within the framework of eternity, we can regularly reassess and refine our desires, ensuring alignment with our evolving selves.

Eternal Opportunities: Every "missed" chance is not lost but merely postponed in our vast timeline, awaiting the perfect alignment moment.

As we navigate through the expansive, ever-present canvas of eternity, melding the wisdom of the Eternality of Personal Time Theory with the Law of Attraction, we are called to manifest with patience, trust, and a deeper understanding of our place in the universe. This powerful fusion transforms our approach to our desires, encouraging us to act with the conviction that every thought, every desire, and every action is an eternal contribution to the masterpiece of our existence.

In embracing this eternal mindset, we are not just passing through time; we are its sculptors, molding and shaping our reality with each intentional stroke, each deliberate choice. And as we progress, let us carry forth the knowledge that within us lies an eternal force, with the power to manifest not only what seems possible but also that which we dare to dream.

CHAPTER 14

Death: The Illusion of a Final Act

Death and the Paradox

Within the pages of our life, the final act is often thought of as death. Yet, when we view our existence through the lens of personal experience, we encounter an intriguing paradox: one cannot experience non-existence. If time and consciousness are bound only to life, then in a profound sense, death is an event that falls outside the realm of personal experience. It's an illusion of a final act in the eternal play of living.

Life as the Only Certainty

The only thread we can trace with certainty is life. From our first breath to our last, we are enveloped in the cocoon of consciousness. The prospect of death then serves not as a definitive end but as a reminder of life's finite nature. It's a concept, a narrative endpoint we never truly encounter, for we will only ever know what it is to be alive.

Time: The Measure of Life

Time, as we understand and measure it, is a property of life. It is the framework within which we organize our existence, celebrate our milestones, and create our memories. The notion of time ceases to have meaning once life, as we know it, concludes. If time is the heartbeat of existence, death may be thought of as the silent space where time's relevance dissolves.

The Finality is a Myth

To consider death the final act is to engage with a myth. For every individual who contemplates their mortality, the actual experience of being ends with life. The self, as a time-bound entity, cannot perceive what lies beyond life because there is no beyond in the lexicon of personal experience—there is no darkness, no silence, no passage of time in non-existence.

Living in Anticipation of Non-Experience

Our lives are often sculpted by the anticipation of death—an anticipation of a non-experience. We construct philosophies, religions, and personal coping mechanisms to navigate this anticipation. Yet, in preparing for an unknowable state, we may overlook the fullness of life. By acknowledging that we will never experience death, we can shift our focus from the horizon of our days to the immediate beauty and potential of now.

The Imprint of Existence

What persists beyond life is the imprint we leave on the world. Our actions, our love, our ideas continue to resonate beyond the bounds of our own time. In this sense, while we will never experience death, our life has the capacity to echo in eternity through the lives of others and the changes we effect in the world

Confronting the notion that death is an illusionary final act compels us to re-evaluate the essence of our fears and hopes. Recognizing that we will only ever know life, and that time is a construct within it, liberates us from the shadow of non-existence. It invites us to engage with life more passionately and wholeheartedly, to cultivate presence, and to treasure the continuity of life as the only true eternal experience we will ever have. Death, in this light, is not a doorway to eternity, for eternity is here and now—the unfolding present that is perpetually ours to experience.

CHAPTER 15

Embarking on Your Eternal Journey: A Guide to Integrating Eternality into Daily Life

From Understanding to Embodiment

While understanding the Eternality of Personal Time Theory is the first step, true transformation emerges when this knowledge is lived and breathed daily. This concluding chapter provides a comprehensive guide to seamlessly integrating the principles of eternality into various facets of your life.

1. Personal Reflection: Recognizing Your Eternality

Begin by grounding yourself in the realization of your eternal journey.

Journaling the Eternal Self: Set aside time daily or weekly to pen down your reflections on time, existence, and self.

Meditative Insights: Practice guided meditations that focus on the concept of timelessness and eternal presence.

2. Relationships: Building Bonds Beyond Time

The relationships we cultivate can be the mirrors reflecting our eternal essence.

Deep Conversations: Initiate discussions about time, existence, and shared memories with loved ones.

Timeless Traditions: Create rituals and traditions that celebrate the continuity of relationships, binding past, present, and future.

3. Work and Career: Purpose in the Eternal Now

Shifting how you perceive time can also transform how you approach your professional life.

Goal Setting with Eternality in Mind: Rather than just short-term objectives, define long-term legacies you aim to leave.

Mindful Work Practices: Incorporate breaks, mindfulness moments, and reflections into your daily work routine.

4. Leisure and Recreation: Celebrating the Everlasting Moment

Your leisure activities can become avenues to deeply experience the present.

Timeless Hobbies: Engage in activities like reading, art, or music that have a timeless essence and connect generations.

Travel with an Eternal Eye: When exploring new places, immerse yourself in their history, culture, and envision their future.

5. Community Involvement: The Eternal Collective

Being part of a community can amplify the understanding and embodiment of eternality.

Join or Create Eternality Circles: Gatherings where individuals share experiences, insights, and practices related to the theory.

Community Projects with a Legacy: Engage in initiatives that benefit not just the current, but also future generations.

6. Continuous Learning: Knowledge Beyond Time

Eternality also means continuous growth and evolution. Books and Resources: Curate a reading list that delves deep into concepts of time, existence, and consciousness.

Workshops and Courses: Seek out and attend courses that focus on mindfulness, time perception, and related themes.

7. Health and Wellness: Nurturing the Eternal Vessel

Your body is the vessel for this eternal journey; it deserves care and attention.

Eternal Fitness: Engage in exercises like Tai Chi, Yoga, or Qigong that emphasize the flow of time and energy.

Nutrition for Longevity: Adopt diets and eating habits known for promoting longevity and holistic health.

Your journey of eternality is not a destination but an ongoing exploration. By weaving the principles of the Eternality of Personal Time Theory into daily life, every moment becomes a cherished step in this boundless odyssey.

As the book concludes, remember that understanding one's eternal nature is the beginning, with infinite horizons waiting to be discovered. By acknowledging and understanding the infinite stretches of our past and future, we can truly immerse ourselves in the beauty and potential of the present, now and forevermore.

Printed in Great Britain
by Amazon